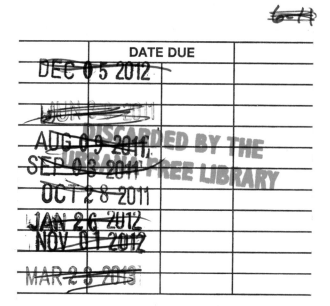

Nocturnal
Animals

Hedgehogs

by Mary R. Dunn

Consulting Editor: Gail Saunders-Smith, PhD

Consultant: Tanya Dewey, PhD
University of Michigan Museum of Zoology

CAPSTONE PRESS
a capstone imprint

Pebble Plus is published by Capstone Press,
151 Good Counsel Drive, P.O. Box 669, Mankato, Minnesota 56002.
www.capstonepub.com

Books published by Capstone Press are manufactured with paper
containing at least 10 percent post-consumer waste.

Library of Congress Cataloging-in-Publication Data
Dunn, Mary R.
  Hedgehogs / by Mary R. Dunn.
    p. cm. — (Pebble plus. Nocturnal animals)
  Includes bibliographical references and index.
  Summary: "Simple text and full-color photos explain the habitat, life cycle, range, and behavior of hedgehogs"—
Provided by publisher.
  ISBN 978-1-4296-5284-1 (library binding)
  ISBN 978-1-4296-6191-1 (paperback)
  1. Hedgehogs—Juvenile literature. I. Title. II. Series.
QL737.E753D86 2011
599.33'2—dc22   2010028663

Editorial Credits

Katy Kudela, editor; Ashlee Suker, designer; Laura Manthe, production specialist

Photo Credits

Alamy/blickwinkel, 7; David Chapman, 13, 15; Juniors Bildarchiv, 17
Peter Arnold/Biosphoto/Ruoso Cyril, 5, 19; WILDLIFE, 9, 11
Shutterstock/Constantine Androsoff, 21, Dan Briški, cover, Morten Normann Almeland, 1

Note to Parents and Teachers

The Nocturnal Animals series supports national science standards related to life science.
This book describes and illustrates hedgehogs. The images support early readers in
understanding the text. The repetition of words and phrases helps early readers learn new
words. This book also introduces early readers to subject-specific vocabulary words, which are
defined in the Glossary section. Early readers may need assistance to read some words and to
use the Table of Contents, Glossary, Read More, Internet Sites, and Index sections of the book.

Printed in the United States of America in North Mankato, Minnesota.
092010
005933CGS11

Table of Contents

Spiny Critters

At dusk, hedgehogs leave their nests to find food. These nocturnal animals are at home in the dark.

Around the world, there are
more than 15 kinds of hedgehogs.
They make their homes in
forests, gardens, and deserts.

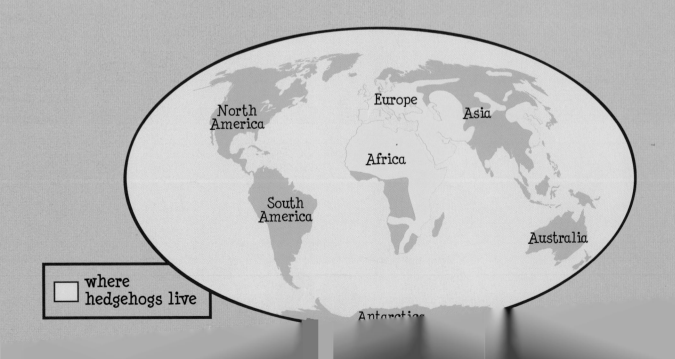

Europe

Asia

North
America

Africa

South
America

Australia

☐ where
hedgehogs live

Antarctica

Up Close!

From head to tail, hedgehogs
grow up to 12 inches
(30 centimeters) long.
They have thick coats
of brown or black spines.

Unlike some nocturnal animals, hedgehogs see poorly at night. They use their whiskers to feel. Their long snouts are excellent at sniffing out prey.

Finding Food

Hedgehogs get their name
from the way they hunt.
They make piglike noises,
sniffing for food in hedges
and other dark places.

Hedgehogs munch on
almost anything.
They eat bird eggs, bees,
spiders, nuts, and berries.
They also hunt snakes and snails.

Growing Up

Female hedgehogs give birth

once or twice a year.

Hoglets are born with

soft spines that quickly harden.

Mothers teach their young to find food and listen for danger. Around six weeks old, hoglets leave their mothers. Hoglets build their own nests.

Staying Safe

To stay safe, hedgehogs roll into balls. Predators can't bite through the sharp spines. Hedgehogs can live up to 12 years in the wild.

Glossary

coat—an animal's hair or fur

dusk—the time of day after sunset when it is almost dark

hedge—rows of bushes or plants

hoglet—a young hedgehog

nocturnal—happening at night; a nocturnal animal is active at night

predator—an animal that hunts other animals for food

prey—an animal that is hunted by another animal for food

snout—the long front part of an animal's head; a hedgehog's snout includes its nose, mouth, and jaws

spine—a hard, sharp pointed growth, such as a thorn or quill, on some plants and animals

Read More

Leach, Michael. *Hedgehog*. Animal Neighbors. New York: Rosen Pub. Group's PowerKids Press, 2009.

Mattern, Joanne. *The Pebble First Guide to Nocturnal Animals*. Pebble First Guides. Mankato, Minn.: Capstone Press, 2009.

Internet Sites

FactHound offers a safe, fun way to find Internet sites related to this book. All of the sites on FactHound have been researched by our staff.

Here's all you do:

Visit *www.facthound.com*

Type in this code: 9781429652841

Super-cool stuff!

Check out projects, games and lots more at
www.capstonekids.com

Index

Word Count: 192

Grade: 1

Early-Intervention Level: 17